Self-Belief

written by
Zanni Louise
art by
Missy Turner

FIVE MILE

Hi, I am Jack.

My name
is Lila!

Hola, I am Mina.

I am Li Wei.

I'm Rosie ...

... and this is Freckles!

A big heart helps you care for the world, care for yourself, and care for others.

But how do you grow your heart?

One ingredient you can use to grow your heart is self-belief.

What is self-belief?

There are many ways to believe in yourself ...

Self-belief is trusting yourself and believing you can do tricky things.

'I'm terrible at guitar,' says Jack, at the end of his first lesson.

'Remember how bad I used to be at jujitsu? Now look at me!' says Mum.

Mum's right. You don't always get it right the first time.

Jack has learnt things before. To swim. To bike ride. To dance.

When Jack tinkers on guitar, it feels like the sun glows in his chest.

I'll get better at this too, thinks Jack.

*Self-belief is giving yourself room to explore.
And space to make mistakes!*

Lila is sure she will win the Science Award. She's the best scientist in her class.

But the glue doesn't stick.

And Dad says she can't take real life bees to school. 'Someone might get hurt,' says Dad.

Lila is very disappointed.

But she thinks about what she's learnt. About bees. About glue. About building insect hotels.

Winning isn't everything. Learning is what really makes Lila happy.

Selfbelief is stepping outside your comfort zone, so you can change and grow.

Mina watches the actors.

'Join us!' calls the drama teacher.

Mina's tummy flips like a pancake. She can't make funny faces or funny voices, or funny shapes with her body. What if people think she is weird?

But drama class looks so fun.

Mina takes a big breath, steps inside and steps outside her comfort zone.

Self-belief is learning who you are and what you're good at. You don't need to be good at everything!

It's Sandy's birthday, and Li Wei, Mina and Jack are drawing him pictures. Mina and Jack are such good artists!

Li Wei scribbles over his art, and starts again.

He throws his second picture
in the bin.

'Good shot!' says Mina.

Li Wei grins.

Now he knows what to
give Sandy for his birthday.

A game of ball!

Self-belief is accepting and loving yourself for who you are.

Mina wishes her hair was curly like Rosie's.

She tries on a wig from dress-ups. She doesn't feel like Mina anymore.

Later, Mina sees her mum admiring herself in the mirror.

Mina's neighbour, Zali, adds flowers to her hair.

Mina takes off her cap. She shakes her hair free. Now I feel like Mina, she thinks!

Sometimes, you don't feel the best. And that's OK! Self-belief takes many different shapes. Just like you, it changes and grows.

Rosie usually loves writing. But today, she's foggy.

Her mind is a blank page. She tries a few ideas. Nothing seems right.

Rosie scribbles shapes while she listens to others share their story.

The shapes become characters. And the characters make Rosie giggle!

'Once, there was a blob. And the blob's name was Harriet,' says Rosie, showing the others her picture.

Believing in yourself gives you confidence to express yourself.

Jack's toes twitch while the drummer keeps the beat. He really feels like dancing. But no-one else is dancing.

Jack springs forward. His feet move like lightning!
He feels the music everywhere!

Soon, people are crowding around, clapping. Some start dancing too. Jack has started a dance party!

Believing in yourself helps you stand up for those around you and stand up for your planet.

Rosie and Freckles' favourite tree is in danger. They could find another tree. But this tree is old. They've seen so many people share special moments with this tree.

Rosie needs to do something.

She talks to Miss Rachel, and Miss Rachel talks to the class. They plan how to save the old tree.

Believing in yourself helps you feel comfortable in your skin, and comfortable in your world. And that inspires others.

Ramadan is nearly over. Usually, Lila doesn't tell her friends. They might not understand why she can't eat between dawn and sundown. Or why she needs to take a day off school for Eid al-Fitr, when Ramadan ends.

But this year, Lila feels like sharing this important Islamic event with her friends.

'I love your festival,' says Rosie, taking Lila's arm.

They give alms to those in need, and share a sweet treat.

Self-belief is trusting yourself, accepting yourself,

and believing you can do things that are hard.

Self-belief can grow from inside. But it can also be built by those around you.

Just as the sun spreads its warmth, believing in yourself inspires others to believe in themselves too.

Self-belief helps your heart grow, so you can look after the world, yourself and each other.

What helps you build your self-belief?

Let's talk about self-belief

Can you remember a time when you believed in yourself?

Monika barrister

'As part of my work, I have to stand up in a courtroom and talk to judges. This can make me feel very nervous, but then I remember I am prepared and have talked to a judge before. This helps me have the self-belief that I am going to do a good job. If you believe in yourself, you can do a good job too.'

Sol case worker

'A big life learning for me is to gradually trust in my capacity to do what is important to me, regardless of the outcome. This means that I can decide to steer my own ship, as well as learn to deal with the rough seas that may come my way!'

Miranda marine scientist

'When I was young, I wanted to do a science project about sharks. Since my school was far from the ocean, they thought I should focus on an animal nearby. My fascination with sharks and belief in myself produced an amazing science project that my teachers and friends loved!'

Bhavni school administration manager

'When I was in my 20s (a long time ago), I taught myself to surf as I had always wanted to since I was a child. It was a time when very few girls or women surfed and I would often be yelled at by other surfers. I would ignore the criticisms as I believed in myself. I remember the first time I ever paddled out the back on a very big swell. I had believed in myself and felt so proud.'

Discussion questions for children

Self-belief is remembering what you've achieved in the past and believing you can do tricky things in the future. It's encouraging yourself, doing your best and accepting yourself for who you are.

- What do you think you did well today?
- Can you think of a time when you tried something new and did your best?
- Is there something you would like to learn to do? What can you already do that will help you learn this new skill?
- What can you say to yourself if you're having trouble doing something tricky? What would you say to a friend if they were struggling with something tricky?
- What is one thing about yourself that you feel proud of?
- Who believes in you? How do they encourage and help you?

Notes for parents and carers

Self-belief is feeling confident that you can learn new skills, cope with challenges and achieve your goals. Self-belief is not overconfidence, but a realistic understanding of your own strengths, capabilities and personal qualities. Self-belief is important for children because it helps them solve problems, persist with difficult tasks, take healthy risks and learn from their mistakes. These experiences will help them become more confident and resilient in the future.

Families play an important role in building a child's self-belief. Children are more likely to believe in themselves when they feel loved, accepted and valued for who they are. Self-belief grows when a child knows they belong, and feels connected to their family and community.

Self-belief is something that grows over time, and can change depending on your child's mood and what is happening in their life. It can also look different for each child. Some children approach new situations with confidence and enthusiasm, whereas others may be slower to warm up. Children need encouragement and patience from their caregivers, as they discover what they are capable of and who they are.

Tips for nurturing self-belief in children

- Support your child to venture outside their comfort zone and try new things, like riding a bike or making new friends. Encourage them to experiment with different strategies and to keep trying even if they make a mistake.
- Teach them how to set achievable goals and break big tasks into smaller steps. Celebrate their achievements, no matter how small. Remind them they can do a lot more now than they could when they were younger.
- Show a genuine interest in your child. Notice and describe what they are doing well, so they can do more of that in the future. Praise them for effort and attitude, rather than results. Let them know it's okay to fail, because that's how we learn.
- Help your child find their strengths and the things they enjoy. Avoid comparisons with other children or siblings, and instead focus on their unique skills and qualities.
- Let your child know that it's okay to feel unsure of themselves. When your child feels frustrated, anxious or uncertain, acknowledge those feelings and help to give them a name. Help your child build skills to manage emotions, so they feel more confident to deal with future challenges.
- Be a positive role model for your child. Let them see you trying new things, encouraging yourself, and being kind to yourself when you make a mistake.
- Notice times when your child needs space to challenge themselves and take risks, and times when they simply need comfort and connection. Let them know you are always there when they need you, and that you love them no matter what.

Dr Ameika Johnson Child Clinical Psychologist

Also available in this book series

Made with love by the team at

FIVE MILE

Alex, Niki, Rocco, Graham, Jacqui, Claire, Amy, Lyndal, Jessica & Emily

Five Mile,
the publishing division
of Regency Media
www.fivemile.com.au

First published 2021

A catalogue record for this book is available from the National Library of Australia

Printed in China 5 4 3 2